D0982458

# THE HOMER MITCHELL PLACE

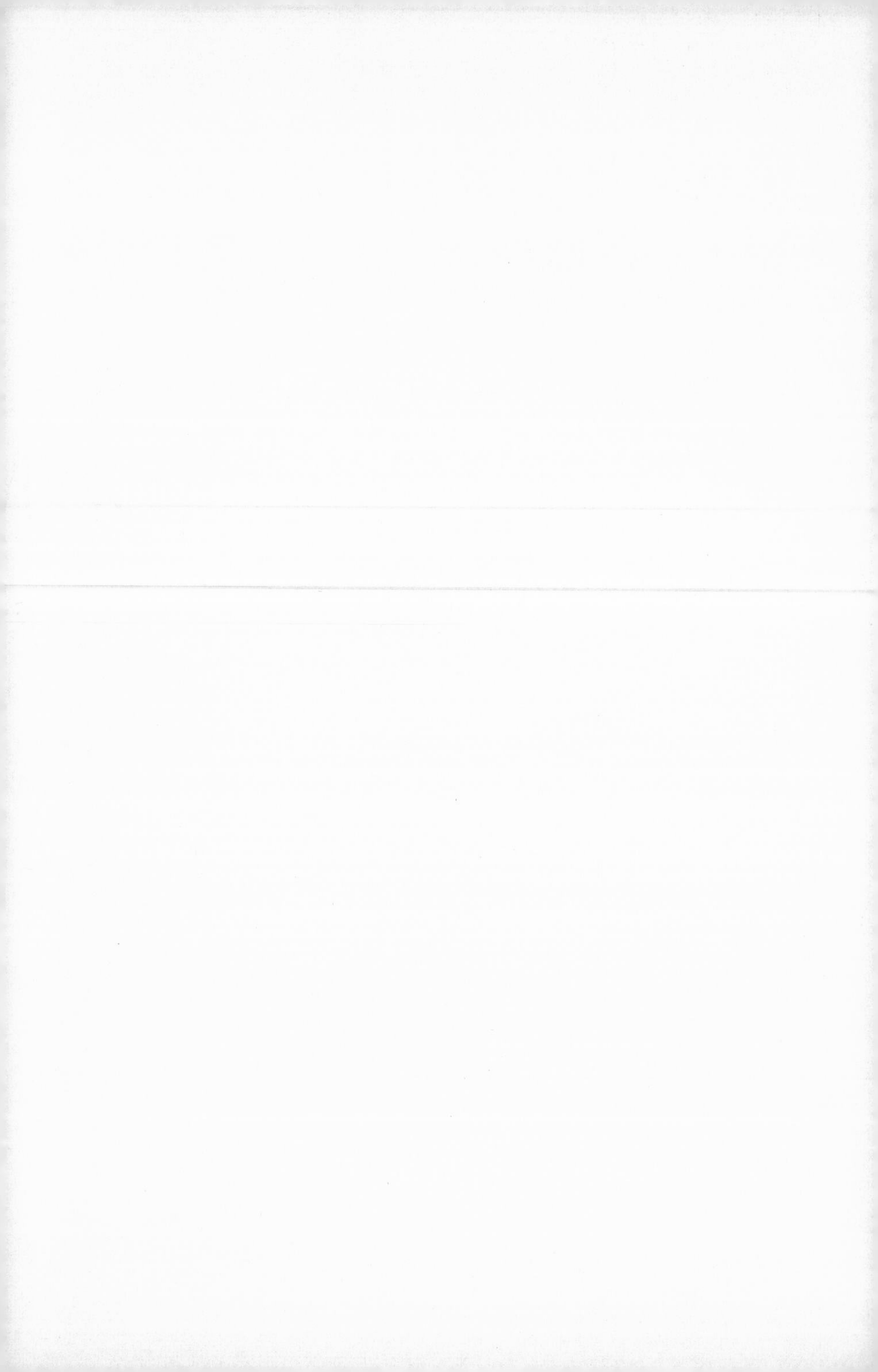

# THE HOMER MITCHELL PLACE ❧ *Poems*

BY JOHN ENGELS



*University of Pittsburgh Press*

Library of Congress Catalog Card Number 68–21624
Manufactured in the United States of America

Grateful acknowledgment is made to the following journals for permission to reprint the poems listed below.

*Antioch Review*: Resurrection. *Colorado Quarterly*: Poem After School. *Commonweal*: Miss Addleman Revisited; After the Grave. *The Critic*: Finale. *The Literary Review*: Weightless in Hell; Horse Hill; Landlord; Petria. *Poetry*: Feeding A Baby; The Fire; Gothic Piéta; The Old Duke; Poem on the Death of the Gardener's Wife (in this volume entitled After the Grave). *Poetry Northwest*: Spring Bass. *The Quarterly Review of Literature*: Confessions of a Peeping Tom; Prodigal; A Dinner Guest; For Suzanne Gross; Upon a Complaint of Silence. *Nation*: A Visitor. *Prairie Schooner*: Bluebeard's Castle (Copyright © 1962 by the University of Nebraska Press). *The Reporter*: For a Christening; For Philip; Cellar Springs in Winter; A Domesticity; Resurrection; Angler; Distances; A Christmas Play (Copyright © 1963, 1964, 1966, 1968 by the Reporter Magazine Company).

In Memory of
Eleanore Perry Engels
and
Philip Stephen Engels

# CONTENTS

## TO MY MOTHER

You will understand me.
Where is the evidence of breath?
The stencilled dovecote tray,
The promised candlesticks?
Your letters are burned.
The bones of your voice
Leap in my fireplace

It does not matter
That tonight your bronze boy
In his coat of crimson lake
Still gestures round the dovecote
On the coffin tray at his gold-powder girl.
My bones will break
To say *love is.*

Mother, I have refused.
Love is to refuse that voice
With every word; it is
The coppery betrayal
Of the blood,
More fiercely cold
Than you have died.

Gold birds freeze in your asphaltum sky.
The boy steps roses on his way.
My hands lie on the bronze
And flowered belly of your grave.
And I have not come back.

*—December, 1967*

# I

## *Hunting Patterns*

## ANGLER

I am back from Bristol, and
The marble sand of the New Haven River
Is drying in my shoes.

And I have left behind me for the fourth consecutive day
Great Browns and Brooks and Rainbows
Lying easy to their color and the head-on stream.

They, by local account, feed
Once a week only, if
In that week has come a heavy rain

To scour the mountain downstream to their gullets.
Now I am back and come
Hungry, without a wife, into a house

That smells of bats and bones and flowered carpetry;
Until next season I rest here:
Below the eddies of my windows hang

Dark fish-shapes grown
Gaunt and savage from
Such hunger as ignores

The tinsel claws and claret bones
My hooks are creatured with.
Mine is the manner of fly-fishermen without fish.

I starve like those
Stone-bellied beasts of all
My strategies, sleep here

In spite of any quarry
Flashing at the hook; and in my house
Dun and imago storm palmer-wound

To spend their wings to gorgeous appetites
Of trout that strike at boulders from the pools.
This August has seen little rain.

## SALMON

This salmon, belly ripped up with my blade,
Bloodies the hand; his gasping eye,
Defined in generation to despise
Any but shape and shadow of the fly,
Pricks in the brain; and tender with
Packed duns and spinners, beetles' zigzag
Legs, a minnow's feathered bones, the gut
Bursts at the merest touch of knife.

Why, if the swollen belly ached from food,
Did he gape in the stiff-finned rush and long
Slant of his feeding run, the taut and final
Water humped and flung, and in the rubric of that
Free rise take and turn with to the grinding
Riverbed the fixed fly coursed of angler,
Stream, and light? O Angler, let the hunting hand
Grow sensitive as that fierce appetite!

## RAINBOWS FALSE-SPAWNING

*for Marvin Fuller*

You call in the news,
Amazed by what you know
And what you saw in the flat of the Falls Pool
In an obliquity of sun without brilliance,
The scarlet spasms of the rainbows finning
Over marble redds in false spawn.

You saw an April-breeding fish grown gaunt
With fall, beasts of color in
The flat of the year, frenzied on stones,
Fins set and flared, in a fire of gills,
Lateral vermilions twisting in
Spring patterns—around you
October paled in milty haze,
And maples burned in clusters orange as roe.

I understand nothing
But patterns of unreason, fall skies
Bright and heavy as an April flood,
A child in an instant dead and out of breath,
A newborn Hereford lying in
A steam of blood in frozen snow,
October ludicrous with color,
Red leaves in a bitter stream.

You call to tell me how
These fool fish spawn in all and fierce
Conviction out of season, gaunt with roe
Under the naked lindens where, in August,
We heard a million bees roar in the sweet twigs
Like a wind, and spent flies eddied
At the roots in yellow drifts—

Now it is time; we ache to know
What cold and color drift the autumn run
And flume of the mistaken blood.

## SPRING BASS

We were late—the bass
Forced up Pensaukee Creek on Friday,
Hung like commas in the curled
Mud-grass, last year

Were early, and
We hooked them, each day
Clumped and scaled our triumph;
In the hand

They died at once, for weak
Air and a foreign sun,
But are remembered:
Had a tiger cheek,

This year again finned there,
And—gone before we missed them—
Tried against the thin stream
And the forcing air.

# II

## *A Dinner Guest*

## THE FIRE

We saw the fire from Ridge Road
And started back, thinking
It might be the Bishop's house,
The seaweed mill, or the
Beginning of the whole town,
As if, burning from one edge
Of center, it had suddenly
Decided to flood its cold boundaries.

At first it was round, like
A young apple, a yellow
Transparent, and then it lengthened
And spread out from the center,
And it was one of those
Circus rings through which
The great pink dancing horses
Leap, never to reappear.

And later, when we were nearer,
It seemed like a giant anemone,
Hungry black at center
And surrounded by nervous
Little fish of flame.
Down we came from the dry ridge.
"Is it the Bishop's house?"
We asked Ringmaster,

Who had been there from
The beginning. "No,"
He said, "I started with
The stables—where are
You folks from?" Well, we
Remembered starting for
The circus on the sea-shore,
But before we could open

Our mouths to answer him
Strong Man ran past, shouting
"The horses are burning up!"
Between us all we led
A few of them to safety.
And when the fire had finally
Burned out three black rings
It melted underground.

I've come to think
That it's still burning there,
And that is why Ringmaster shifts
His feet so daintily, and the Bishop's
Horses are more likely to leap
Than dance at the touch
Of the warm sea on their
Gaily decorated hooves.

## PETRIA

Petria honored the Falconeri Virgin.
Smoke from the bone-heaps
Burning on her altars covered
All of Dublin; and she loved,

From time to time, Gervase
O'Donough of the Spanish Rosary
(A souvenir) and crossed
Herself at every bell, until one day

In serving her fires she scorched
Herself a bit, and he—of a sudden
Flightless and in a funk—
Read her from Compline

Where it says of sacrifice
God has no taste for burning feathers.
Thereafter she
Inclined exclusively to Abbots.

## A DINNER GUEST

Arriving early I prepare to wait for him,
And leave the motor running; on my right
Novena ladies hustle into church.
The windows of the Priory are bright.

And on my left the snow spins from the river,
White upon a vertical of pines,
My harvest of the visible until
White-caped and capped he enters the design,

All head and hands and nothing in between
To leave his tracking towards me, white-on-white.
He sits beside me in the car and says, "If I
Had wit for season, I would fear these nights,

They take such toll of color and of shape
And force me to congruity with storm."
At home a pine-fire falters on its ash, or seed.
My headlights blaze; the car is warm.

* * *

At home the snow is heavy on the rooftree, and
Advances up the sidewalk like a smoke.
He says, "On such an evening we should bake a trout,
Drink wine, reflect upon the joke

The winter makes our bodies be; and long
For spring and time to thump our mud
Into a sign of living, long to tap
The sharp roots of our breath again to blood

To flower on the bedclothes while we sleep."
At ten I take him home, and home again I douse
The smoking fire, and all night I dream
The bright snow's slow invasion of the house.

* * *

I should have said to him, I lose
All voice for simple language in this white;
The season asks for silence, a free giving,
But your gift was color as you walked last night

That cold of street to meet me, and
Were lost to season but for hands and face.
My ungloved heart cried out for home to see
Snow flower on your eyelids as I traced

My pattern back across the river; frost-weed
Clattered at your heels, and on the walk
I saw your footprints holding shadow like a darker ice.
We should have taken fire for our talk.

Instead, not fearing what cold season ached in your design,
That it exacted from you what of color is your share,
Before my pine-fire burning rose and gray
You spoke of how, once from the Abbey's freezing stairs

Clad in a scarlet cassock you had heard
The cries of spring swans come to the melting lakes
For feeding fat again before they flew
Their orange beaks northward, and how in their wakes

You prayed to answer any question *love*!
But I would give burnt sacrifice of my two-measured tongue
Against dark mornings of such wings because
They leave the sky brilliant with departing, and with sun

Or sequence for my body, and it dies; and darker
Than your footprints shall have gone
From Abbey stairwell, or from Priory
And towards my fire across my frozen lawn,

The snow tonight falls like bones burnt
Of feathers spent into the airs
Of autumn gardens and neglected lawns.
Against such season I have said my prayers,

But waking from a perfect dark of sleep have heard
The wild lacery of snow that roars
Like apples in their steady fall across the heavy planet,
And sung like a grave old man of my long hours.

* * *

We walked together till another time.
I took him home at ten to please the Prior,
And waved him into snow across the street; our hearts
Are eaten this late season to a taste of fire.

## GOTHIC PIÉTA

Plucked by their gold twig-fingers from
The flat bronze sky to feed
The hungry season of their love,
He is the last fruit of the eyes
Weathered like green winesaps
Gathered from under some dying orchard tree
One season after snow.

Having felt sun
Under the shadows of the brittle leaves,
Their cheeks are like smooth bowls
Scattered with apple twigs,
Broken after the threefold branching
Cut fork and flower
Out of the glittering blade of space
That gathered them,
Under the towered walls and tomb,
To breathe the bronze sky of Jerusalem.

## RESURRECTION

Thank God he died so quickly!
It was some time later that He waked again
In Market Place, where he had fallen.
And it was night. The city filled with rain.
Our shutters fell. We had gone home
To honor our fish-fallen and to breathe
The warm green of the supper's steam,
Thick claws jerking on the fire, unsheathed
For us. And we could not believe it

When He swam against the door,
Showed us His scars, and settled in.
God, we heard it all a thousand times
And more, and from politeness let the fires thin.
The night rose, deeper than His voice
And crested, splintering the bells and bones
Of our old town, and leaving scars along the stones
In Market Place for all the years our suppers cindered
And we watched our fires burn to whale bone.

## RESURRECTION FROM THE COUNTY HOME GARDENS

Because good God grows weary of His dead
In proper season it begins, with pigeons
Flaring up from muddy lawns, that these
Old County men are taking color in their dust.
Bats flurry from their bare-boned nostrils,
Grass is grubjaws at their toes, the petalled
Skulls grow cavernous, they feel the first
Breath tear again like troutbones in the throat,
And they go blind of sky, but bound
Such strength of pattern that they do not grieve
They died nailed down by garden roots and fishes' spines.

Today is spring: the spider-footed herons freeze
In beach pools, and the kitchen serpent
Turns its notice to the sparrow's nest.
The earth whirls like a child's hat
Whole lengths of blazing streets; now these
Old men, who wearied of the holy season at
Their risk, permit themselves no sleep but shout
And clatter down their corridors.
Their graves are flooded, salamanders flash,
Fish swim in eel-mottled skies, the sun
Is bloody beaks and tongues of pigeons at their eyes.

It is a new time and an empty town.
These old men have so intricately spun
These many years their beards and bones, and prayed
In proper praise of time and name, how have
They meant, except each ghost at last
Contredanse on carpets, jig in purple bags,
Fly loud and blazing in its breath to flower on the bone?
Each knows the grave roots rip the belly if he rise,
But thinks perhaps from such extravagance
Of agony no creature dies.

Today the garden elms still shake
With voices of old men who undertook
In time the constant and proved worship of
Arrangement; today they spin
Like bonestorms through the gardens to
The western lawns, and none remain
For news and prophecy.
Old men, if love struck any pattern to your bones,
Then now should be the long dream of that juncture.
Remember us you have not seen for years.

## WEIGHTLESS IN HELL

We are weightless in Hell, we two,
Mere skeletal illuminations holding to
A gold-and-ruby flesh and hue.

These vestibules of blackness
Where no one was before we came,
They are the very worst, and less

In making *black* a not too unimaginable name
Than in not telling which is finally best,
The gold-limbed doll or antique ruby eye

That wonders coldly where we've come from,
By which holy water we were blessed,
Away from which pale sky

(For color is but one
Sad weightlessness in Hell, a slow warm sun
Of no attraction towards which we lightly run.)

# III

## *A Complaint of Silence*

## PAINTING-LADIES

They measure me against the light.
Inexpert white-and-blue, I crowd
My veins, for they have little time.
Then all at once they cry aloud,

Pleased with the spectrum of my breath.
(May light confound me to their eyes'
Distract of shape; I stand and pose,
Assume the seasonal disguise.)

They sketch my figure from its fall.
Their gentle brushes diagram me
Out of sun; at length they pause:
The first shape from transparency—

Light entering an edge of flesh,
Dark in the tense blood, filled and burst.
I breathe from their dozen eyes, and in
Their point of dark I am the first.

## HORSE HILL

Shut out from the stable
Warmth of steep Horse Hill,
I saw in their thick manes
The summer's residue,
And the grass greening
Between their dry teeth.

I lay still, and I
Was never cold.
Had they seen me
With their crystalled eyes,
Or come much closer,
Hooves delicate in rime,

I would, I think, have spoken,
Not caring whether it might
Frighten them away,
Or let the cold into my mouth
And freeze me into
Their transparent weather.

## THE OLD DUKE

He found the water cooling his dry lust
Too soon absorbed into the season's dust,
Bestockinged lace-throat with a dripping quill,
One hillside and a pond, two daffodils,
And merriment in right proportion; to be just,
His reason was not brittle, but was pleased
To see the flowers wilting at his yellow door
And flattened out beneath his children's knees,
Crushed thin and white from leaf to floor
And perfect dust to make his duchess sneeze.

# FOR SUZANNE GROSS

Your poems insist we perish in
Particularities of color, fire,
And creaturely articulations such
As joint and bell the onyx-eyed bullgods
And dewlapped kings who feast upon
The creatures that you leap and dance
To your geometries, like brocade
Hunting-beasts in tapestries; and are,
By this, in proper praise
Of name, and the betrayal of its terms.

You clearly trust in sequence,
Substance, and the polity
Of Christ as Landlord, bishoply of flesh;
Still you betray—to write
Of Pasiphäe, Baluba carvings, Eve
In heat—of self a Paraclete:
Antiope gone light of wax-white bone
As any Ammanati nymph, more joyful
For God's gravity than lived, and saved
In golden-hatted sons who are
The service of a spouse both elegant and fierce
And grown too old for simple nakedness.

## UPON A COMPLAINT OF SILENCE

*Do Thou, who givest speech to the tongues*
*of little children, instruct my tongue.*
(Aquinas)

His tongue done up in periwig and powder
One sings his measure as a poet's feet
Stamped dust before blind Œdipus,
Petulant and proud; my measure, too,
The twinfold darkness of the sealed tongue.

If one could only speak and find it done,
Then what of the riches of the God-struck child
Who takes a child's voice into his children's rooms
Against their copious eloquence of dream?
The dancing fat monk died in straw

Still squeaking from the sweet pipes of his bones
The cries of copulating giants scared by thunder,
While the old man's body, blue as blazes,
Weary on the rooftops, slept the weight
Of its great chaining tongue away.

## FINALE

His last trick is the attitude of flight:
Hooves flashing for balance a hundred feet
Over the blazing ring, he freezes at Ringmaster's cry,
Forelegs in a taut hook, head and neck side-wrenched

And heavy mane flaring the color of the ribboned dark.
Against the dark his eyes burn bright as early season
Planets, and he sees his shadow poise: the lights
Crumple his wings against rough canvas, and below him

Half the world spreads gold as sawdust, and
The circus rings his body, scarlet pompoms for his breath,
A silk braid twining in his veins—Ringmaster laughs:
"The trick's a sparrow's wings caught to the back

By golden wires, hooked in the flesh and blacked
To match the dark!" The children gasp. He spins a moment
Slowly on his point of dark, and falls before
The drums can roll him slowly down again.

There is applause before Ringmaster whips his ghost away:
One circuit of the ring, a bow, and then the Dancer
Pins her sharp feet to his back and rides him out
Into the stable and extending dark.

# IV

## *A Domesticity*

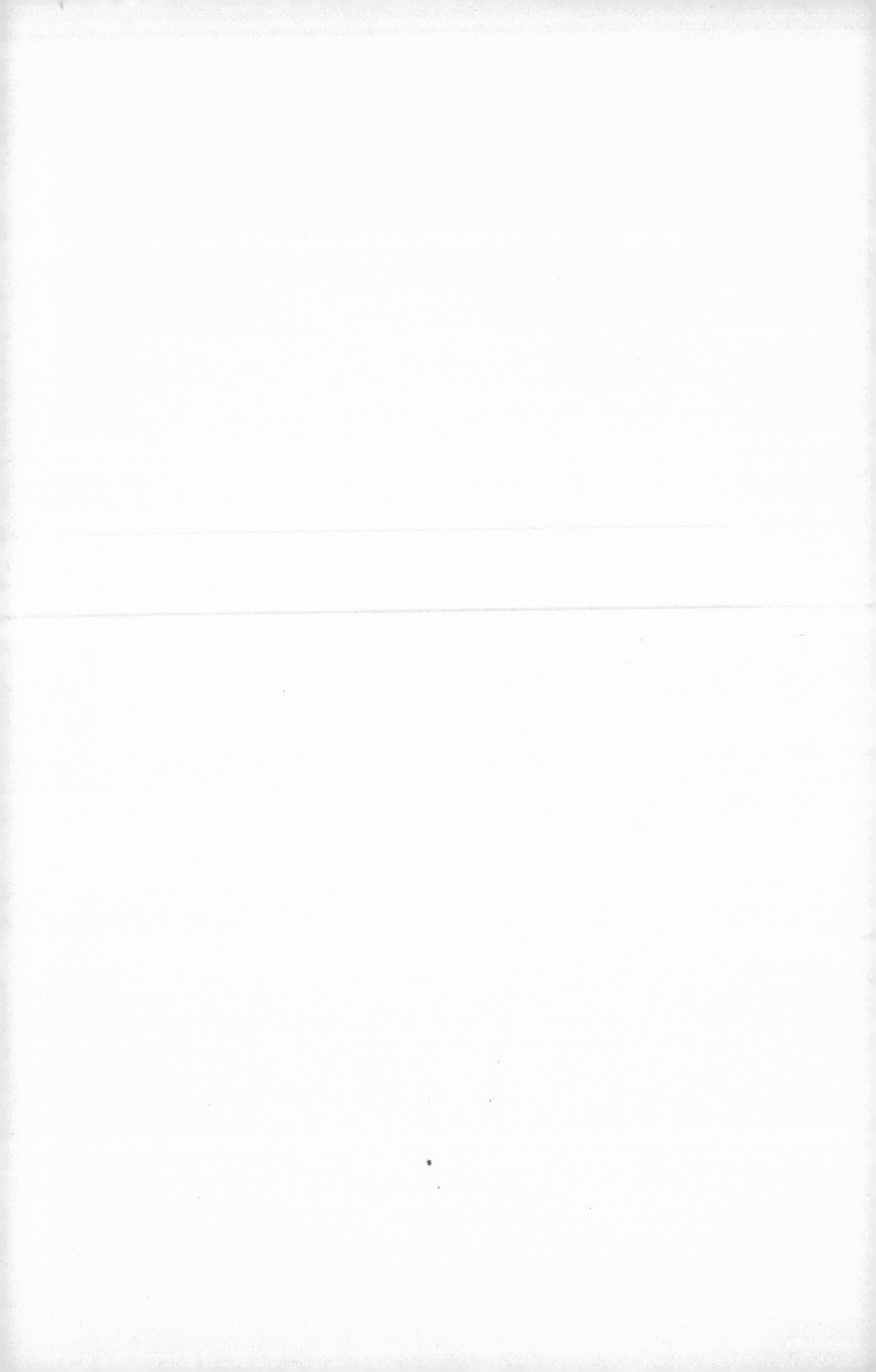

## SISTER VINCENT COULDN'T PRAY

Sister Vincent couldn't pray
And told us so each school day.
We prayed for her; in every prayer
We never doubted our despair.

Bribed once with convent apple tart
I quicksilvered her Sacred Heart;
She wore it blazing on her gown
Until in time it tarnished brown

And she grew stern and red of eye
But did not weep; I wondered why
And wonder still—she'd paid me well
To wear the brightest heart in Hell.

Growing old and somewhat stout
Sister Vincent went in doubt,
Once she'd found the heart could dull
And apples thunder in the skull.

Sister Vincent tried to pray
But died at Lauds one school day.
I have not prayed since I was young
But tasted apples on the tongue.

## MISS ADDLEMAN REVISITED

Mourners come and go, the family stands
In corners of the parlor, shaking hands: I wait
Among the raftered shadows of your vestibules
In line, at length respectfully to view
Your straightway bones, and leave in my good time.
A child makes croupy coughing in her hands,

And from the stairwell windows to the West I see
Where up on Schoolhouse Hill the maples dry
In winterbud, beneath an Easting sky; the halls
Are stacked with Crisco tins for kindergarten clays.
I step the attic stairs through nested hay
Your old man laid ten years ago, and died.

Your graves are elsewhere, here was where you lived.
From Schoolhouse Hill I hear the playground bell
Or merely slate scrap rattled by my feet.
Miss Addleman, I mutter at your sheets: I fear
My diverse bone distracts and teaches me
My chalky heart is monitored too well

To dare again, Miss Addleman, as in those years
You made me wait the noontime recess out
Upon your creaky office cot for fear
My doctored heart might die of play yards, all
The fierce attentions of the dying child
Pinned down to sleep beneath your chalky shawls.

## A BARBER'S CALENDAR

My father found on Western Avenue
An old scab barber with a name like ours,
And cheap enough to matter, so that for
A sequence of some Saturdays I went
To breathe warm atmospheres of *Three-in-One*
And bear a bee-sting buzz at neck and ears.
He sheared me to the bluestriped towels
And barber-ticking bibs; my father,
Waiting, did not watch, for magazines.

I watched the *Copenhagen* calendar down which
Two bearded tramps ate lunch along state roads
That tapered, leech or lancet, Maine to Arkansas
Into a single letting of the sun.
Now, of the two old unshaved men who lunched
Along those roads, the younger one, who sought
Inheritance, has smothered on his beard,
Or choked in stairwells, long grown old
In hairoil-smelling houses of the fathered rich.

I have dismissed him long ago.
As for the other, orphaned to his yellow stick
And slung bandanna, he is still
As silent as when Engle clicked his shears
Like voices at my head to drown
The step and speech along the brush-bound roads.
What barber would not weep with joy to apron him
To comb and brush and shear him clean,
Lay bare his neck to prickle in a father's hand?

How many Saturdays of never sleeping from
My powdered, freezing neck I might
Have run before him as he picnicked, drawn away
The thousand barbers chasing after him,
And left him staring after us into
That single narrowing of May and January roads
That speared clean through the paper, paste
And lavatory lath, and found
No picnic weather in the alleyways.

Instead, each Saturday I tramped back home
Light-headed, North and East on Western Avenue,
My father ringing with saved pennies at my side
To spend on haircuts, and in growing rich;
Or possibly for picnic weather; or we might
Feed orphans from that charity for grace,
And watch them pity us grown old in calendars
To beard and thatch, and wary of our barbers till
The highway trims and scissors on our necks.

## PRODIGAL

Hunting fields through stubbles of late wheat
Four pheasant's eggs were crushed beneath my feet.
By noon the grass had rubbed my bootsoles dry.
I'd thought perhaps it was not time to die.

One war I phoned my folks to hear them say
"Come home, the war is over now." But they,
Grown old in hearing, had put on the light
And left the house; the phone rang half the night.

Tonight I seem to starve, and suck for air.
I crush a child's bones in stepping where
The dead lie stretched like feathered beasts upon
My muddy gardens and neglected lawns.

The bedroom light still burns, the windows craze,
The doors stand open, all the chimneys blaze,
But cock-birds strut the kitchen floors and crow.
What question's like an egg-shell in the throat?

## A DOMESTICITY

In spite of table, child and wife
We drove for greens one Christmas day
And tried the stomach bitters in
Some Polack tavern on the way.
The forest pine was dry and thin;
We swung the heavy brushing-knife
And skittered ice-pucks on the lake
Until too late; in time we came
Back home to find our wives awake
We had abandoned while we played,
So danced set measure in our shame
At child asleep and supper made
And spoiled upon the table, grown
As cold as wind across the ice
Had played and tasted at the bone.
Grown seasonal in artifice,
We lock our doors; the children dream.
If angry women wept alone,
We played at cutting evergreen
In our good time, and have come home.

## A VISITOR

We rented here, the only house
Was the village madman's, very cheap.
Being strangers, we tried
Not hearing what the neighbors told:

Locked up tight for fulfilling
A few town maids, he never
Came around.
We used the place, and one day

In a seethe of July dust, all
Tags and tears, the town dogs
In a fury at his heels,
We found him grinning at the door,

As we discovered we
Had often feared. "Welcome,"
He said. It appeared
We were from the very first

Not far from his thoughts,
Never wholly absent from his heart.

## FALL MOVE

The first day renting in this house I'd found
Where in the cellar neighbor kids had cooked
In a rusty skillet over paper-ash
The bones and feathers of a rooster's wings.

Then, stepping carelessly from stair to stone,
I felt my heel skid and saw the eyes
And bulged guts grained with cellar loam,
All but the knotting tail a long time dead.

It was the Landlord's salamander, come to feed
On spider casts and catch mosquitoes from
The fouled cistern, growing bold and fat
From hunting basements where he'd died at last

Of tenantry about the Landlord darks.
All night the crushed tail coiled and pulsed
As if it hunted where it lay; I knew
Because I'd done it he was dead, and feared

That having killed a Landlord's beast,
Now heaven help me, I must pay
Or watch the Landlord sell the house away.
I packed up skillet, ragged wings, and all

My sleeping children from their beds
To other Landlord rooms; it was
Because I had not feared his darks I was surprised,
Before this fearing mostly what I'd owned.

LANDLORD

The two young ladies in the rooms below received their calls
On Friday afternoons O'Donohue was not about.
They muted their teacups and were careful not to shout,
And shortly after ten would murmur in the halls
With all their young men, make them wind their mufflers tight
And pack them whispering away till Friday next should fall.
O'Donohue was never home before they doused the shilling light
To dream black pudding, Guinness, and a mouse between the walls.

Those Friday evenings when O'Donohue was not at rest
Among us and his careful landlord walls, I waited for the young men
Eagerly: their voices teacup-thin up through the floor until at ten
They left more silently than they deserved, or we, and we undressed
His beds and made ourselves into them, shivering with fright
Until our Landlord should come home again; ah, we were blessed
Those Friday days when they were finally whispered out of sight
Into the muffler-grey and chilling streets; we lay abreast

Above each other and the shilling-meters measured out our sleep
More steadily than all the young men stepping bright down
Grafton Street
By now, as Landlord forks and spoons; and they had voices sweet
For dreaming to we dreamed for hours, waiting from his deep
Dry breathing beds for old O'Donohue come home to smell
out guests
And breathe around our doors all night, and finally climb the steep
Stairs that we followed Fridays, hurt and angry; Landlord, how
we blessed
Your party house for you, and held the shadows in it for our keep.

Come back from where it is that you have been, away from us
Each Friday with the image and the duty of your walls
Conveying you, to purchase us away from bed and serve your halls
And tuck away your silver and your fragile cups, and fuss
Us back to sleep again. O'Donohue, where is it you have been
This party day away from home? And, Landlord, why so curious?
You've frightened our bright shadows all away again
To city-ward, down Grafton Street, rejoicing in the muss

They've left behind them; Landlord, there's no hope in you,
Nor trust; wherever you have been—on Clontarf Strand
Counting the houses and the toadfish swarming on the sand
Like tenants, or in Francis Street, or up on Holyview
Rejoicing in the rooftops—rest assured the party will be done
And over with and all of us quite safe asleep when finally you
Come home to count our beds. Only the young men, every one,
Are thieves, and leave your house behind them for the clue.

# BLUEBEARD'S CASTLE

Like a mountain straining from a weightless plain,
Bluebeard's castle anchors its keen point
Deep into the heavy planet's core
And warming fluid of the landlord's brain.

Beside the floating drawbridge a great crowd,
To take advantage of a reasonable price,
Has gathered, and maintains itself in weight
Uneasily, not yet accustomed to the proud

Release its Lord's estate accords; they've come
For seven Sundays, fearing less the screams
And blood that some expected, or the dreadful
Lordly apparition, than the equilibrium

Of threshold lands that they inhabit.
They balance teetering in trees
Until the rooks, which have been flying a great height,
Descend along their song and mark officially the Sabbath.

At the extremest range of song they are invited in.
The Lord himself appears, wearing heavy shoes,
And bids them welcome, handing everyone
A lucky key and program for the tableaux; once they're in

They're taken to the heavy doors and shown the flowers:
Sprays of bloodwort for the children, for their fathers
Beds of merrybelles and quaker's-wives,
And finally, after several hours

Spent browsing in the armories of glass and china blades,
Among the ruby coffers, in the cruel room
Sleeping his sly ladies' empty beds,
Shortly beyond the landscape with its bloody shades

He gathers them together at the Seventh Door.
"The ladies are not dead," he says, "I've saved them for you."
And they listen for the sound of real breath
And women splashing on the naked shore.

## CELLAR SPRINGS IN WINTER

In the cellar room dug out
Last summer, first a moisture carried
Up the walls and dried away
Into a blotched and estuaried

Map-edged stain upon the stone;
And then there grew a small
Run stirring up the gravel
Of a far-back corner floor; it was

For weeks a sound I thought
Merely blood in an ear-vein
Beating when I stood to watch
The push of my white breath

Onto the clay-cold air.
And now, something of a welling,
A currenting, a live stream
Grown and noisy in a single night

While I slept and heard
Nothing; and now,
Because the water surges so
In one new, dark and freezing room,

The rooftree thunders overhead,
The pinelog joists
Are shredding to the hand,
The spider-warrened walls

Could slide and heave; I carry
All that darkness where I am
Through stable boardfloor rooms,
And do not breathe

To hear below the soft slip
Of the mud floor falling in
And down to heavy gathering.
All day and night I hear

The cellar springs run underneath;
Not in the memory of any here
Has cellar water run
When snow was on the ground,

And ice is damming up the eaves.
This water is one gathering
From hill land that I own;
Behind the house the land I own

Goes dry to flood me while I sleep.
I do not sleep; the cellar stone
Runs stronger every night; beneath
My heavy house and hill

The planet's ruptured dome
Is bleeding to the cellar hole,
The one owned room in all this house
Where breath was visible.

## CONFESSIONS OF A PEEPING TOM

The flowerbed commands a striking view;
A drying Indiana lawn walked on near midnight
Makes the sound of straw-soled slippers in a bath:
Such is my single strategy of innocence, that if
The naked neighbor girl should drop her towel to listen at

Her blinds, to her it might seem something more of dignity,
Perhaps a freshly-bathed and breathy fat proprietor
Of gardens taking air therein to ease the belly, all
His women safely wed and in their rooms, and cautious
Of their window panes; I am intrusive of her garden

And squat among the poppies for a peek before she spends
The shadow of her belly to the landlord's bed, and I am left
To breathe a garden air in all its dark.
Then it is difficult, having slept naked for a wife,
That, home again, somehow the blood is louvered from its light

In prints of street headlighted on the rose-leaf wall,
The rumble of hot-weather fans, the breath of pillow
From another room; and every night comes Landlord with
A breath like shrubbery; tonight the neighbor girl undresses
To a dream in which I peek between mock-orange and firebush.

She shyly locks her blinds too late on house and lawn,
And then, plump-breasted shadow on the glass, she sleeps
To pray a penance for the village burning in my hallways;
Shortly my house untombs charred skeletons of lawns
And racks of maidens trapped in the flaming fodders.

## POEM AFTER SCHOOL

With his yellow cap tipped forward
He runs home through the empty pasture,
The tall grass bending over on each side
Making yellow veinworks and bright
Corridors for him to fill up
With the warming light of his breath.

What remains of the schooltime air
Weaves into the grass: fathers,
Lemonsweets, suppers waiting. And think
How he screams when, not quite home,
He feels the hunting-shadow's weight.
Night comes earlier on school days.

Again and again he is almost home,
And I have to search in the grass as if
I expected to find yellow cap-feathers,
Burned-out books, or some evidence of breath
I may have passed before dark came
And the moon rang me home like a bell.

## FOR A CHRISTENING

The Eagle father tests his child
As child of him, by the sun.
And child of no betrayal is
That fledgling which, despairing less
At pain than poverty, goes blind
Of its obedience.

This morning we must face this child
As Eagle child, fearful at
Its test of sun stares body blind
Against that blazing raptor, lest
He sacrifice inheritance.
And fearful of our child, ask

What risk took Simeon, grown old,
To feel the stooping at his eyes
Of heavy birds, contemptuous
Of sons burned sightless, seeking heirs?
Recall how much more quickly did
The Child plunder at his eyes.

## 5:30 A.M., FEEDING A BABY

Cow-breath and pigeon-feather, dust
And pollen, paper-smoke, the hair of bulls,
Sunflowers rotting in the swelling sun:
I strain my breath into the shadows I awaken from,
And think how it begins: hands clean as grass,
Tongue thin as willow leaves, and bones more delicate than wings.

Today is spider-clouds behind the trees,
A beast-emblazoned sky, and ruddy stare of tiger's-jaw;
Everything recedes from
A garden-colored dark into
The hallways of my ruined household
Where morning comes through leaf

And shadow with a giant step
To warm our image in its iron frame.
Even a small house echoes to the sun.
The child has filled himself drowsy
On the milk of houses half back into color.
He is the stranger met along my corridors,

Bare to the flower-jointed bones.
*Cheerup!* the early bird,
Archangel ruined, great
Ragged wings drooped against the sky—
I favor color to forget
The family dark.

In the late of this new dark what light is left
Is shrunken like a child's hand, and blood
Beats rising on the ear as harshly as an edge
Of ragged feathers; what light is left
Squeezes colder than the veins can stand,
A ghost of dream conserved another cycle.

Around the corner of my house where wind
Breaks like a muddy fist, the hot beast slides
Across a yellow field with grass like splinters,
Pausing only to sharpen his claws on some
Snarling child, or roar for the sweet milk
That will quench his thirst after a weed-dry winter.

Here is the blind and tiger-jowled child
Propped in the curve of a snowhill, sucking ice;
And over this blunt cornerstone of houses, there
His breath heaves in some heavy ordering,
Perhaps the beast-smell in his point of dark,
Or the grass is rattling like spears aimed anywhere.

His skin prickles for the brilliant claws.
The water freezes on his chin.
What shall I pray for out of such a dream?
This morning I am apple-child starved to seed,
Recalling the sear of my sweet fire through the tree,
And in whichever eye is dream for me?

## A CHRISTMAS PLAY

They act this play out in a northern cold,
Four angry children fighting over parts.
One, weary at the Inn-door, has become
A raucous Magus who forgets his part,
And will not sing, or will not sing the words,
Resenting he must give up what he is
To what he never was or will be; in the end
The Virgin has become a Shepherd Boy,
And Joseph bellows *glorias* upstairs,
Sent there to be an Angel, but born obstinate
In being; one won't play at all,
But sits and strokes the plaster Ox which stands
Four-square beside its empty stall and chews
A year's dry upstairs-closet dust; the night
Is thickening with snow, and none believe
They take their part to any end, but are
What blood of season makes them out to be,
Virgin, Angel, King, or bitter Spouse.
They fight to play whatever part they take; none fight
To play a mute child unattended in the straw,
But watch the snow dust on the windowscreens, and taste
A dust of Eden thicker than the snow.
Beasts roar outside, grown frantic with the cold.
Their voices freeze in gardens on the glass.

# V

*For Philip*

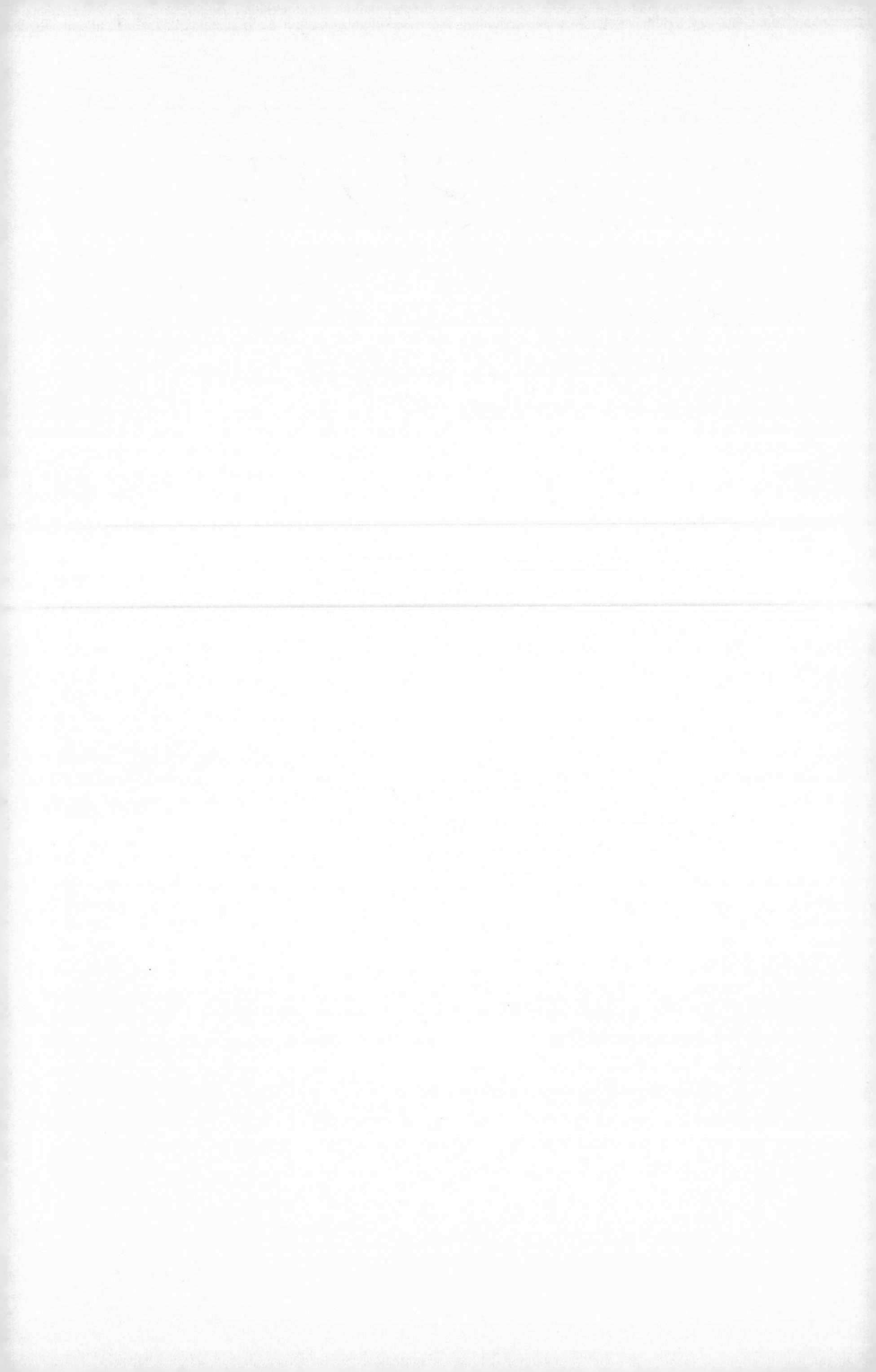

# FOR PHILIP STEPHEN ENGELS

*August 23–October 24, 1965*

Swarming by your head
Red plastic butterflies
Danced patterns on their strings
Because that night you cried

And would not sleep; and I,
In my dark room, rejoiced
To know that bright beasts moved
Measured by your voice.

The sun came red as wings
To fix the swimming dust
In all our rooms; my son,
Your caught voice moves in us.

The house drowns in its lawns.
We watch the morning sun
Thrust deep into the sky
A boned and bloody tongue,

And in that roar of light
You sleep; above your head
The blazing wings grow dull
And larval on their threads.

You were no voice at best.
I measure what I tell:
The housed and swallowed bone
Grows hollow as a bell,

The breath swims in the throat,
The sun rings in the sky;
What color we remember
Burns inward from the eye.

## DISTANCES

It is the final grief, how color echoes on the eye
In distance, and its cold perspectives.
I see a child in a red hat and jacket walking down
The lines of the severe fences
Through a snowy field and spare bristle of weeds
Till his brave color dances
Random on the retina, and blots; the eye reflects
Back travelled distances
Of its cold fields, and color dies at the farthest range
In the green pine peninsulas.

Ghosts walk in color where the brain most dazzles white
And strains at distances the eye refused,
Fearing most that fierce geometry that angles sight
To the utter point the blood eludes.
O our children die beyond our seeing always,
In the green trees, in the frozen roots,
In the fenced fields' extremest ranges always,
Having outwalked color, having moved
Beyond the shadows of the neighbors' farthest trees, until
The eye breaks on the fearful residues.

# POEM AT DAYBREAK, BEFORE THE GRAVE

Half-turning to the window lights my eye;
Snow runnels on the sulfur piles at dawn,
And from the elms, intaglio on sky,
I watch the rake of shadows down the lawn

And hear the rooftree roaring in its bark
As if I had awakened it to dark
Of leaf and flower, or some such dispraise,
And later than its branching could be drawn

Or figured for the sight again; such brawn
Of elm-bone braces in my house, and groans
Its grave tune to my point of days,
The rotting spine leafs violently in praise,

The fingers flower inward on the bone.

## THE GRAVE: 1

Perched on the barn sill, racketing at dawn
To see the red and wattled sun come up again,
The furnace cockerel grows raucous of his blood.
He sang you to your last and barebone name.

But you cried sequence like this flaming beast
Who calls the day in, or the day gives voice;
It is the born bone you took balance on to sing
The bright and fiercest measure of our time.

## THE GRAVE: 2

Frost in his nostrils, ice between his teeth,
He takes for breath the shadows from
His frozen skull each slow first coming of
This season; and it seems today
The whole air of the heavy planet breaking
Into cold that I am the one he left,
And of us both most speechless.

However long he lay for finding and
I looked my reason, then I should have died.
I have no way but waiting in
His simple measure now; breathe in and out,
From North and South there leap
The child's beasts; at noon the sun
Bursts like a royal fox onto the sky.

I am in time to see his eyes
Blaze from the grave like
Beast-tracked surfaces of lakes the wind has scoured,
From whatever season it has come
To set his breath this rigid gesture from design.

## AFTER THE GRAVE: 1

He returns to his house as if
To step out again into the vacant yard
Or onto the frost-heaved walk, as if
To walk in the orchard under the purple crabs,
Knotting in their roots the broken roots
Of his late garden, were tomorrow.

He returns from a long trip he remembers,
And forgets the flowers have not blossomed yet,
But only the amber walls light up tonight
To make his shadows cross like phlox-stems
Broken; *here*, he thinks, *I stop*: shaped in the glass
At the end of the corridor, bending his jewelled hands

Like a clown's gloves, fingers to boneless palms
In circles for an eye to peer out through;
Knee-to-chest, left foot turned toeing out,
One arm extended and a bleeding tongue
Dangling a bell at the tip to ring the mirror down,
And let him look both ways. Light breaks again.

Spring drifts in the shattered garden, and for him
Departing to return is to recall the shape of his hands
Among flowers, smudged green, smelling of marigolds,
Palms shiny and smooth, hard as the warm hall-glass
He mists when he speaks; and to recall the thrust
Of the buckling earth that first cold season.

## AFTER THE GRAVE: 2

I have forgotten, it was time or not,
And we had come this distance from that place.
The late streets burned with ice, the car was hot,
Yet season drew the white breath from your face

And froze it to the windshield, leaf and flower,
Stem and pod; but we were coming near
And late—for all that proof of breath (God knows the hour)
We stopped someplace to scrape the grown glass clear,

For whether we had come or we had gone
From home or host it still remained to see.
The winter cracked and flooded on the lawns.
Our clean glass caught moon-shadows from the trees.

The clear grain of the white road turned to mud,
The roadsides leaped and hollowed; we were home.
We saw the garden greening with his blood.
The child's hands rake and ravel at our bones.

## TWO CHILDREN

I am beset by cellars where dark water rots
To stink in hallways; and I have begot
By some confusion out of some fierce game
One child who died, another who did not.

I have a living child whose greenstick bones
Sprout from my fathers' tillage and my own,
Or we were the soil, and gave enough to die,
And she is branch and flower of the stone.

She rackets in my rooms, her voices mock
The raucous bellings of the household clocks.
My cellars flood; this living child breathes
To make my rounds, unsnapping all my locks.

In time at last the narrow body grieves
At flood of season; twigs dam up the eaves,
The maple's dead, the mountain turns to stone.
My lot is littered with the bones of leaves.

My son is dead. My daughter lives with me
Where I have lived not having come to see
In bonfires blazing on the sodden lawns
The charred and sweetened honeycomb the bone can be.

## THE HOMER MITCHELL PLACE

The mountains carry snow, the season fails;
Jackstraw clapboard shivers on its nails,
The freezing air blows maple leaves and dust,
A thousand nails bleed laceries of rust,
Slates crack and slide away, the gutters sprout;
I wonder do a dead man's bones come out

Like these old lintels and wasp-riddled beams?
I ask in simple consequence of structure seen
In this old house, grown sturdy in its fall,
The brace and bone of it come clear of all
I took for substance, what I could not prove
From any measure of design or love.

Or is it rather that he falls away
To no articulation but decay,
However brightly leap the brass-hinged bone,
Beam and rafter, joist and cellar-stone?

# COLOPHON

The poems in this book are set in ten point Palatino, leaded two points. Palatino was designed by Hermann Zapf, and aptly named for the Sixteenth-Century Italian writing master. The version used here is the German Linotype cutting.

The book was printed by Heritage Printers, Inc., on Warren's Olde Style antique wove paper.

The design is by Gary Gore.

*Pitt Poetry Series*

James Den Boer, *Learning the Way*
Jon Anderson, *Looking for Jonathan*
John Engels, *The Homer Mitchell Place*
Samuel Hazo, *Blood Rights*

I. Mary Roy McD.